CW00551089

HOW TO FIND AND SUSTAIN A GREAT RELATIONSHIP.

Dr Grace Anderson

DISCLAIMER

DISCLAIMER.

This report is only a guide. There is nothing here that should be taken as a prescription or advice. You can choose to use any of the information in this report or you can choose to ignore it all. It is entirely up to you.

The author has written this guide only as an educational and informative material. She cannot be held responsible for any results or for no results at all.

By reading this report, you agree to indemnify the author of any issues that may arise, if you choose to implement any of the suggestions.

PREFACE

HOW TO FIND AND SUSTAIN A GREAT RELATIONSHIP

This book is a simple **Dating Guide** and **Relationship Guide for Men, Dating and Relationship Guide for Women, and Dating and Relationship Guide for Divorcees. Adolescents and Young Adults will also find the Online Dating Guide very useful.**

It is also a very useful **Online Dating Guide** on **how to find love online.**

These days, finding true love online is very difficult, because of the proliferation of Dating Sites and Dating Apps.

Some people are online looking for temporary connections, perhaps, sexual connections only. However, there are other people online, who are seriously looking for the **"One True Love"** for them.

My Book will guide you in knowing what to do. You will get the chance to think seriously about why you want to go online to find love, and when you do find the "one", what to do to make sure that you are compatible with that person.

You will also learn some tried and tested strategies that will enable you keep that relationship "sweet" enough, to lead to a permanent relationship. Once you know why you are actually looking for love online, it would be much easier to focus seriously on doing the right things to sustain that relationship, after you find the "One".

The following topics are covered in some detail:

- **ARE YOU LOOKING FOR LOVE?** - Search your mind and be honest with yourself before you start searching.
- **IS ONLINE DATING SAFE?** - We look at strategies that will help you keep safe online and avoid scammers and time wasters.
- **WHAT ARE YOUR INHIBITIONS?** - Are your fears holding you back? Do you think you are too ugly, too fat, too old, a failure because you were once divorced, etc, to find love? I show you how to overcome your inhibitions.
- **ARE YOU COMPATIBLE?** - Compatibility is the key to a great and happy relationship. I show you how to determine whether or not your newfound love is actually compatible with you and how to walk away from that connection if you feel it is not working.
- **COMMON PROBLEMS IN RELATIONSHIPS** - Every relationship has problems. We will explore some of them.
- **HOW TO KEEP YOUR RELATIONSHIP HAPPY** - I give you several tried and tested strategies to help you keep your relationship very happy.
- **ARE THIRD PARTIES CAUSING YOU PAIN?** - Some couples unwittingly let a third party take over their relationships - telling them what to do and what not to do, etc. I give you strategies to help you keep the busybodies in your lives out of your private business.
- **SPIRITUALITY AND RELATIONSHIPS** - Many people are lucky to find the partner who are spiritually matched to themselves. But what if your partner does not share your spiritual beliefs? Mayhem could ensue! I share some strategies that you can use to diffuse any spiritual misunderstandings.

- **CONCLUSION - I share some of my Online Relationship Courses - on my Amazing Success Academy: https://amazingsuccessacademy.com - with you, and offer you a chance to book your First Coaching Session with me for free, if you need further help, with either finding Love or retaining your current relationship.**

You may be happy to know that I am a Master Life Coach and a Relationship Coach. Many of my Clients have found the strategies discussed in the book very useful. So, grab your copy and let me know later, how it has have helped you.

You can access my Life Coaching Website here: https://www.lifemasterymasterclass.com if you need immediate help with your relationship issues. Thank you!

CONTENT

INTRODUCTION

<u>How to Find and Sustain A Great Relationship.</u>

Relationships can be wonderfully fulfilling if you were lucky or clever enough to find the right partner for you. They can also be a nightmare if you hooked yourself up with the wrong person.

This eBook is only an introduction on how to find success in your relationship. It does not claim to have all the answers.

However, it does contain several strategies that have been found to help lots of people in the past, so, if you put some or many of them into practice yourself, you could find them very helpful.

Several strategies listed here have helped the author herself to find her true love online after a divorce. Try out the strategies diligently. With a lot of patience and a bit of luck, you might just find your true love!

CHAPTER 1.

ARE YOU LOOKING FOR LOVE?

Let's assume that you have now decided to find love because of one or all of the reasons below:

1. You are lonely and you need a companion who can share your life with you.
2. You are getting old – maybe over 25 years old and you think it's time to settle down.
3. You recently broke up with your partner and you need a "better" person to replace him /her.
4. You have a need to get married because of your religion, your parents' hassling you, and your clock is ticking.
5. You want to have children before it's too late.

And so many other reasons.

This little eBook will guide you on where and how to find love. It will also offer you some success strategies that you can apply in order to find the right person.

If you are already in a relationship, some of the success strategies here will also help you if you apply them with diligence.

Looking For Love in all the Wrong Places?

You probably remember that really old song called **"Looking for Love in All the Wrong Places."** This could describe the search that many people go on to find that elusive love that they've been hoping will find its way to them. There are too many people in the world that do keep trying to find love in all of the worst places they possibly could. If this is you, it's possible that you don't even realize you're doing it. What you probably do realize, though, is that you want to keep striking out over and over again in the game of love.

Bar Hopping.

Are you hoping to find that special connection with someone by indulging in **bar hopping**? While that almost always works when it comes to **one night stands,** you probably won't find your true love in a night club. That's not to say that it won't ever happen, but the odds are usually not that high when it comes to long term romance and forever after relationships. It's fun to go to out dancing and having a great time. Just keep in mind that having fun is usually all that happens in a night club.

If you're trying to find someone to form a true relationship with, it's good to, sometimes, get to know that person from the inside out. In that way, you can discover what sort of person he/she is and whether or not you've got anything in common.

Online Dating.

Many people choose to do this through online contact. This can be done through chat rooms as well as the explosion of online dating websites. These sites offer the opportunity for people looking for potential partners to scan personal profiles, list their own, and match up with website members that they seem compatible with. **This is a method that has worked successfully in a lot of cases.**

Match -Making Companies.

In this same vein, there are also match making companies that take charge of connecting people with those that are most compatible with each other. Of course, these companies cost a lot of money to sign on with them. For many people, though, there can't be a price put on the chance for a healthy, loving and long term relationship. Some people save up to pay the fee so that they can join one of these services.

Clubs and Communities.

You can also join various clubs and community groups, like Meetups etc, where others have the same interests as you. These are the very places that you'll find someone that can end up being the one you've been searching for all this time. Many communities have singles events and groups that you can join so that you can interact and become acquainted with other singles that are also looking for love. **This method can be more effective than those you pay for.**

Just keep in mind that when you're looking for love, you need to pay close attention to the places you're using to hunt. That can tell you a lot about what your chances of success will end up being.

Finding A Boyfriend or Girlfriend Through Online Dating.

Admittedly, the Internet has opened up a lot of options for single people. However, not only single people have benefitted from this easy and unique way to communicate with other people. Married, and otherwise attached, people also now have a way to discreetly meet like-minded people for fun and games without any strings attached. But if you're single and looking for a real boyfriend that's not already with someone else, you now have lots of ways to do that. One of them is through a reputable online dating site. There are ways to be successful in doing things this way that will save you time and energy.

First of all, when completing your profile, be very specific about the type of man/woman and relationship that you're looking for. In that way, guys looking for one-night stands or a sex buddy will probably pass up your profile.

Honesty is Key.

Be honest about who you are and what you're about. If you have any fetishes that are important to you, it's probably a good idea to mention those, too. You won't be wasting any time on guys that you have no future with.

It's also good to decide what is NOT important to you. In that way, you can open up the door to guys that may not have all things in common with you, but you'll find that there are enough good things that you both like that it makes it worth a try. If you're still having fun with him after a couple of months, there's no need to even consider the things that you may disagree on.

Profile Script.

While writing your profile script, be honest and add a touch of humour. Make it interesting to the reader. Mention what you are passionate about and also things you really don't like, in a humorous way. Dating Sites usually give the opportunity to check the things you like or can't stand – eg **"Smoking", "Drinking alcohol", "Sports", "Reading", "Religion"** etc. Make sure you choose the ones that apply to you. If you lie about these options, you may be surprised that the only people who respond to your profile are the wrong ones.

Profile photos.

If you are a woman, post decent photos of yourself. **Avoid putting up NUDE OR PARTIALLY NUDE PHOTOS on your profile.** They show you up as "loose" or "immoral". Also, post one or two pictures of you not wearing make-up. Guys know that women typically only post the very best and most glamorous pictures of themselves, so it's kind of hard to know what she really looks like first thing in the morning. If you take a picture of yourself when you're not in make-up, you'll still get responses. Most men want a REAL woman, anyway, not a mannequin.

If you are a man, putting up nude photos of yourself will put really serious-minded women off completely, particularly ladies who are looking for long-term partners or husbands. They prefer to get to know you first as a responsible and likeable "person", before wanting to know how big or small your "manhood" is, if you get my drift.

Also, put up other pictures of yourself in different parts of your life. For instance, if you like biking, post a picture of yourself on your bike, wearing your biking gear. Post a picture of you on vacation in your favourite spot. If you like going out at night, put up a picture of you wearing full make-up and dressed to kill. It's important to give a full scope of the person you are, and pictures are excellent ways of doing that.

Delete Irrelevant Responses.

Something else you can do is to immediately delete any responses that seem to completely and totally ignore what your specifications were. Now if you do get some responses from very cute and likeable guys, but they're not looking for a long term relationship or they're not into your particular fetish, you can simply send them a polite email back thanking them for their interest. You don't have to be mean about this but be firm that you're looking for what your profile says.

These are ways that have worked out for many people when they were actively seeking true, romantic friends. If you haven't had any luck so far, try doing things this way and see what happens.

CHAPTER 2.

IS ONLINE DATING SAFE?

New Age Dating Methods.

Dating is one of those things that everyone has done at one time or another. Back in the days of high school, dating was considered fun and exciting to all. But those days came to an end once you got married and grew up a bit.

Now that you have divorced or are single again and you are tired of living on your own, you might want to consider dating again. So, how does an adult, who has been married for almost 20 years, go about dating in this day and age? Some things have changed greatly since those early days of a movie and popcorn date.

The first thing you are going to notice is technology has taken over the clubs, bars, and fairs that people used to go to in order to find a date in the first place. Facebook and various other social networking sites have pretty much taken over that aspect. Don't forget about all those dating sites that you see commercials for on your television, either. Computers and dating are starting to go together like sugar and coffee these days and, because of that, you are going to have to change your game up a little bit.

It is really difficult to convey emotion when you are typing to someone on a computer. Remember that when you are saying things through an instant message or email, you are going to have

14 | Page

to be fairly specific so you don't end up scaring that potential date off. What might be a funny opening line in real person, where they can see the smile on your face and the hint of sarcasm in your words might just end up offending someone who is simply reading it online. Always take that into consideration when you are trying to find a date through a social networking or online dating site.

FAKE PROFILES.

You should also be aware that the person you are talking to may not be the person they are portraying themselves to be. There have been numerous accounts of guys acting like women and vice versa just to start up a conversation with someone as a joke. You might also find that the strapping quarterback or energetic cheerleader turns out to be a 350-pound man named Judd that lives in a trailer behind his mother's house. Make sure they send you a picture with a hand-written note to you with your name on it to be sure.

Dating in this type of a technological age is something that a lot of teenagers have no issues with, but anyone that has been married since the advent of the home computer, can remember what a modem sounded like while connecting to AOL, and loves the old drive-in movies might have a difficult time adjusting with how things are done these days. Don't worry, though. If you are lucky, the person you are looking to date, will feel the same way you do and that will just give you something to talk about while you are waiting for your movie to download onto your phones.

SCAMMERS.

Among the Fake Profiles are the notorious scammers usually from Ghana, Nigeria, and other places. They are usually made up of gangs of men using Model Profiles of young women to dupe unsuspecting men. Some other male scammers use fake photos – photos of genuine white men found online and claiming to be them.

i)**Catch them out by asking for direct phone calls with you** – not Skype messaging or WhatsApp Message where they can use some fraudulent technology to dupe you of your money.

ii)If they refuse to call you on your phone for a direct chat so you can hear how they sound, stop responding to their messages – change your email address and phone number!

iii)**Another note of warning: Don't let their 001-… phone number fool you.** That number with an American code could be fake. They are not American nor are they in America. They may have told you they are American Soldiers, Doctors, Pharmacists, etc and put fake photos of American men on their Profiles. Request a Facetime chat on the phone with them.

iv)   **STOP contacting anyone who tells you a long and woeful story of how they need money for a flight ticket to visit you, to get their family member out of hospital or to pay a tax bill etc.** Remember, these are scammers, they will sweet-talk you into parting with your money. **DON'T BE FOOLED OR SCAMMED!**

v)   **BE VERY CAREFUL!**

FIRST MEET-UP

If you have managed to find a genuine person who is interested enough to want to meet up with you, great! But where should you meet up? My suggestion is in a public place, and never in a seclude area, nor your place or his place. Meet up in a Restaurant, a Pub or any open place with many other people. And at the end of the meeting – GO HOME! Don't follow that person to their home. Then take some time to think about that person – your conversations, the vibes between the two of you – was there any "spark" between you? Do you think you might be compatible? The second and third meetings must also be in Public places. Never visit your new-found date in their own homes until you are sure you know their values and can trust them.

Always tell someone at home who you are going to see and give them that person's photograph and phone number to be safe.

One-Night Stand Persons.

Don't Let Yourself Be A One Night Stand.

One-night stands have been indulged in ever since men and women realized that sex is fun. The thing about these one-night stands is that they're usually fast, simple, fun and have no strings attached. There's another thing about them that many people don't fully understand until they've had one or more. **One-night stands can be very unfulfilling and leave a huge black hole in your emotions.** This is the reason that, if you're looking for more than just sexual release, you're going to want to avoid them at all costs. **In short, don't let yourself become a victim of one-night stands.**

As many nightclubs are pickup scenes, unless you stick to those places "where everybody knows your name," you probably don't want to get too heavily involved in going out to them. **The**

exception would be if you're going out with friends or you have a date. Then, it can be fun to hit some of the larger clubs for drinks and dancing. If you go alone, however, you're putting out signals that you're looking for a quick hook-up that can only lead to a one night stand.

It seems that men enjoy these encounters more than women, although there are plenty of women that aren't interested in long term attachments. These women tend to go out deliberately to find men that are willing to have that fast encounter and then be on their way. Whether women like it or not, they're more at risk of becoming victims if they're not careful. So, the location of the encounter can be anywhere from a stall in the restroom, the back seat of a car, or up against a wall in a back alley**. It's very unwise for a woman to take a stranger home for sex or to go to his place.**

Something else you may want to think about when it comes to safety is that there are still **various sexually transmitted diseases** that you don't want to catch. While none of them are pleasant, many can be treated and even cured. **There are a couple of them that won't kill you, but they'll never go away.** Then, you need to remember that at least one can kill you. Not everyone is going to be responsible enough to use protection during these encounters. So that's definitely something to think about.

If you're not someone that really wants to make a lifestyle of one night stands only, then you need to take precautions and ensure that doesn't happen. Don't put yourself in positions where you may be tempted to engage in one. Put that energy and effort into finding the right dating site or company that will help you meet someone that wants the same things as you do. Always remember that a one night stand isn't going to bring you the relationship that you want. Anytime you feel particularly needy, it's much safer to keep your nightstand drawer outfitted with just what you need. In that way, you won't be risking your life or your self-respect.

Is Online Dating Actually Safe?

"Is online dating safe", you ask. "Aren't the online dating sites made up entirely of perverts, sexual predators and weirdoes in assorted shapes and sizes?" The answer is, yes, there could be, but not as many as before. It is up to you to be very CAREFUL in making your choices. It's as safe as you make it using common sense and sound judgment.

Use the same caution that you would when meeting any stranger. Don't give your real name, address or phone number until you feel safe doing so. Don't rush into a face-to-face meeting until you are confident and then make the first meeting in a public place and during daylight hours.

It's true that online dating, while in its infancy, was only made up of perverts, sexual predators, nerds and weirdoes, but that is no longer true. It has become the main tool of the single person in every developed country in the world. Forty million people can't all be wrong. Ask your girlfriends if they have ever used online dating or are using it now. If they are honest with you, most of them have or are now members of at least one online dating site and maybe more than one. It really is the way to go to meet eligible men who want to meet you. It doesn't matter what any of your numbers are...like age, height, weight or income either. Somewhere out there in the big wide world there is a man who will like you.....then love you....and think that you are beautiful and desirable.

Give it a try…Mr/Ms Right might be a few mouse clicks away.

What Are the Odds of Finding Mr. Right/Ms Right Online?

The odds of finding your "soul-mate" online are a lot better than you may think. It doesn't happen for everyone, of course, but it can happen for you. The world of internet or online dating has exploded over the last few years.

As our lives become busier and busier, we need to make better use of our time and energy in our search for the one man who will make our lives complete.

The old saying, **"You have to kiss a lot of frogs before you find a princess"** is no longer true. Why kiss frogs when you can read hundreds of profiles and look at the pictures that go with them for a small monthly fee? That saves time and money…not to mention lip burn.

In Chapter 3, we will look at Possible Inhibitions that can keep you from venturing into finding a date that could become your beloved life-partner.

Chapter 3.

WHAT ARE YOUR INHIBITIONS?

Are You inhibited by Your fears?

Are You Sabotaging Your Own Love Life?

Are You Picking the Right Guys?

If nothing you do seems to turn out right, it could be because you are not picking the right guys. When this keeps happening and there's no visible reason for it, you may want to consider that you're ruining things all by yourself. There are various ways that this can be done without you even seeing it.

For one thing, you always pick the wrong guy. It may be that you have Bad Boy Syndrome, which keeps you from ever choosing the right man or woman for you. Do the guys you date all seem to treat you like something they've scrapped from the bottom of their shoe, yet you still stay? It may be that you give all the power in a relationship to every guy you get involved with, which means he dictates how the relationship will go. Maybe, you zero in on guys that aren't emotionally available, or they just won't commit. While these guys may be exciting, unpredictable and phenomenal in bed, they're not going to stay with you, and you actually know that from the onset.

Another way that you're putting obstacles in your path to true love is by staying in bad relationships too long. This goes for both man and woman. These are the ones where you KNOW you need to leave because you're not getting what you deserve from it. The sad thing is that you come up with all the excuses in the world as to why you're staying in the relationship. You tell yourself that it will get better or that he'll change. Love doesn't justify being unhappy. **Yes, love is very important, but you need other things to make a relationship successful. Things like respect, compatibility, honour and communication are just a few. When there's real love in a relationship, all of the rest will be there as well.**

Fear.

One of the things that keep people tied to a bad relationship is "fear of loss and of being alone".

One of the biggest ways to sabotage your relationships is when you base your decisions from a place of fear. Rather than doing something because it's what you want, you do it because you feel you MUST. You're afraid that if you do what your intuition is telling you to do that you won't have the relationship and life you truly want. You understand that by confronting things that upset you or make you unhappy, then you may have to make some hard decisions. So, you calm down instead of speaking up. The important questions are avoided because you're not sure you want to know the truth. That's why you bury your head in the sand, rather than acknowledging all of the warning signs around you.

You owe it to yourself to be honest with your partner about how you feel. You need to communicate with each other more effectively.

Have You Been Damaged by Your Last Relationship?

Most people feel "damaged" after a relationship they thought would be perfect for them failed to work. It is very easy to lose your self-esteem and self-confidence after leaving an abusive relationship. Abuse can be both physical and emotional. There are people out there who thrive on belittling their partners in order that they themselves could feel "superior" to their partner.

If you have had the misfortune of being in such a relationship, it is hard to get rid of the mental damage that that may have caused you.

Seek Therapy.

It is a good idea to seek counselling or therapy from a qualified practitioner so you can begin to get over the hurt and damage caused. You will find that unless you are able to get rid of the hurt caused by your previous partner before entering a new relationship, your hurt may create problems of trust for you in your new relationship.

So, my suggestion is to get counselling or therapy and give yourself time to heal before moving on to a new relationship.

Do you Feel You are Too Old to find love?

Are you 30 and over? 50 and Over? 60 and over?

Don't worry, there are people out there on Dating Sites that want people around those ages**. I am speaking from personal experience here. I found my current husband at age 69 and he is 8 years younger than me!**

A lot will depend on your own self-confidence and the kind of person you are looking for.

It is true that some people – men especially – go out there looking for women who are at least 30 years younger than they are!! Talk of "fathers" wanting to marry girls their own "daughters' ages"! They are sick!! But, if that the ladies themselves want, for example, those seeking "Sugar-Daddies", then that's ok! As long as the two people get what they want, there should be no problem.

Life isn't fair. Men get all the breaks. You've devoted all of your 20's to getting your career off the ground. Not that you haven't been dating...you have, but not seriously. Now here you are...30 something or older and there is no long term relationship in sight.

You can actually hear your biological clock ticking. You have a precious few years to find a man to fall in love with, make him fall in love with you, get married, and have a baby or its lights out. You already know all of the men in your social circle. Not that they aren't nice guys...some of them...but none of them are your soul mate. What's a girl to do?

Advantages of Online Dating.

With Online Dating, you have the opportunity to read hundreds of profiles and look at hundreds of pictures in search of that "someone" that will be right for you. Maybe he will live in the same city you do...maybe he will live across the country or even in another country altogether. You are not limited to only those men that you come in contact with personally. The possibilities are almost endless.

You can decide not to give out your real contact details until you have seen the person in public places a few times in order to ensure that he/she can be trusted and also that you are compatible. If you stay sensible, you will be safe.

"Beauty is in the eye of the beholder" is true. What is considered beautiful in one part of the world is completely different from what is considered beautiful in another part of the world. It's even different from one part of this country to another.

Find an online dating site that suits your needs. Write a great profile and post a flattering picture. Start contacting eligible men on the site. Mr. Close-enough-to-perfect could be a few mouse clicks away.

Chapter 4.

ARE YOU COMPATIBLE?

The Importance of Compatibility in Relationships.

One of the most important ingredients of a successful relationship is that of having something in common with your partner. It may not seem so important in the very beginning when you're still in that afterglow of lust. Everything is beautiful and wonderful with your new love at that point. However, as things start to cool down just a bit, you'll start to see just how much having things in common with someone can mean.

Consider that you're someone who loves mystery and scary movies. You love a great psychological suspense plot as well as supernatural ones. Your partner, on the other hand, prefers action movies where there are heists gone wrong. As long as something gets blown up and there's plenty of fighting and bloodshed, he doesn't care WHAT the movie is actually ABOUT. Neither of you can stand the preference of the other one. You end up going to see movies separately or watching them in different rooms of your home. That's not really quality time, is it?

Suppose one of you loves to read and also loves to discuss the books that you've read. As you try to talk to your partner about the latest book you've just finished reading, he's nodding at what you're saying but, at the same time, his eyes are glazing over. You know he's not really listening because he's actually bored to death.

Then, there's the area of activities. He may love to go camping in the wild, but your idea of camping is to stay at a rustic mountain cabin with all of the amenities. You may like to go hiking or biking, but he loves an afternoon of skydiving. Clearly, there are some vast differences in this area of your relationship.

Now, while there have been rare occasions when a relationship has made it successfully even though the two people involved had absolutely nothing in common; that just doesn't happen all that often. For the majority of couples, having at least a couple of big interests in common that they can enjoy together is pretty important. While an initial physical attraction may have brought them together, what will they do when they find they have nothing of interest to talk about with each other?

Find out Your Date's Interests and Values.

There is nothing that creates loneliness more in a relationship than the two people in it not having some common interest.

Let's Look at Values.

Your values are the things/ideas that you feel are really important in your life – like Your Religious beliefs, Your Idea of Comfort, Your Idea of a "good" person, and Your idea of fairness – what is wrong or right, etc. Put bluntly, values are subjective things – they are created by you to help you survive on this earth. They also come from what you were taught to be right and wrong in your childhood.

If you and your partner disagree about whether or not God exists, you will have a real problem about how to bring up your children, or what to teach them. If only one of believes in a certain value as being important, the children may be confused about what values to hold sacred.

That is why one of the first things you need to do when meeting someone new is to get into a conversation about what each of you enjoys doing, what your values are and how important these values are to each of you.

Hobbies.

It is also important to find out your partner's hobbies. If he/she is into mountain climbing and you're terrified of heights, chances are that you should simply find a polite way of disengaging yourself from this person because you're obviously wasting your time as well as his/her's. It's not rude to move as soon as you've found a polite way to do this, because you're actually doing both of you a huge favour. If you continue the conversation, the attraction may keep growing and you'll find yourself involved in a relationship that has little or no chance of working out in the long run. Instead, keep looking around for someone with interests that match yours. You'll be much happier in the end.

CHAPTER 5.

COMMON PROBLEMS IN RELATIONSHIPS.

Relationships Are Never Movie Perfect.

Now that you have the **"partner of your dreams", how well are you too relating since you moved in together or got married?**

Have you yet discovered that the "infatuation" that drove you to believing you were meant for each other has now worn off, how are things between you two, sincerely?

Unfortunately, relationships portrayed in movies don't often play out so beautifully in real life.

Unless you've been living under a rock during the last few years, you're aware of the *Twilight Saga* in both books and theatres. While this is a totally captivating series of books as well as movies, *Twilight* has probably done more damage to relationships single-handedly than anything else in existence. Girls see how Edward treats Bella and they all want their boyfriends to treat them the same way. What they're not getting is that, in real life, there are no guys that treat their women the way that Edward does.

Edward is a fictional character created by a woman. That should explain everything to those mooning females out there that dream of the day that their Prince Edward will come. Now, please don't misunderstand me. *Twilight* is easily one of the most entertaining book series to come along in a while. If you were to ask your partner as a woman, why he is no longer as romantic as he was when you first started dating, I bet he would say, without even blinking, that: "It's simply not fair to expect real flesh and blood men to act the way that a supernatural character in a book acts".

How and when did you fall in love? Was it a wild-fire affair? If yes, you have been fooled by your hormone – oxytocin - which makes you fall-head-over-heels in love – It's call infatuation! Seriously ask yourself how you can fall in love with someone you don't even know well? The main answer to that one would be that you're not in love with this person. Rather, you're infatuated with him. He may be gorgeous to look at and you may feel an instant lust for him, but it's not true love.

The fact that Bella's infatuation continued to grow and become love is something that just rarely, if ever, happens in real life.

Women must stop trying to turn their men into Edward. That's not going to happen anymore than most women would turn into Bella. Sure, women love their men, but would any of them go to the extremes that Bella does in these books? Probably not, when you really think hard about it. She's not any more real than Edward is. Real people need to start understanding that.

Couples have romantic and fulfilling relationships all the time. They just don't usually go the route of the plots in Twilight. If you're in a relationship or you want to be in one, **be realistic**. Look for someone that you can get to know and someone that will want to know who you really are. There's so much more to a person than the way they look, and you cannot hope to know someone simply by looking at them.

Communication is Key.

There must be talking and interacting. **Communication is key.** It is the only way to find out what you need to know about someone and tell if you want to be in a relationship with that person. It doesn't happen any other way. In fact, if you do try to pin it all on how attracted you are physically to someone, you'll find out just how disappointing a relationship can be in the end.

Mr. or Mrs. Perfect Does Not Exist!

The sooner you realize this sad fact, the sooner you can get on with finding Mr. Close-Enough-To-Perfect. Prince Charming, riding on a white stallion, lost his way, or found Princess Charming and got married on his way to your castle, doesn't exist!. **Get over it and get on with it.** You ARE going to have to actively seek the man of your dreams and you won't find him hiding under your bed. You already know that he isn't among the men that you are acquainted with so, now what? Online dating is "what".

Tools for Resolving Difficulties.

The Importance of Communication.

I can't stress enough the importance of effective communication in helping to resolve difficulties in relationships.

People communicate in different ways. Some people are naturally good communicators while others are not so blessed.

There are also differences in communication styles between extroverts and extroverts.

The most effective way of communicating with your partner is using the **"reflective listening technique"**.

What is Reflective Listening?

Simply put, it is a communication style that effective parents use with their younger children.

If you tell your five-year-old how to cross the road on the way to school, you would possibly say it this way:

You: John, remember to look left, and then look right before you cross the road. Make sure that all cars have stopped before you start crossing the road. Is that clear?

John: Yes, Mummy.

You: So what did I say to do at the Zebra Crossing before you cross the road?

John: Mum, you said once at the Zebra crossing, I must look left and then right, and only start crossing the road when all the cars have stopped moving and are waiting for me to cross.

You. Great, John! That's exactly right!

You could say to me: *"But Grace, we are not babies!"*

Yes, I get that. But the one thing that causes friction in adult relationships is the fact that the other partner is not always listening attentively when you speak to him or her. It takes patience and interest for you to listen to your partner. But if for some reason you or your partner is upset about sometime, it could be because of an issue at work, or something you said earlier, chances are that he or she may not have "heard" or "understood" what you said. So

HOW TO FIND & SUSTAIN A GREAT RELATIONSHIP – DR GRACE ANDERSON

it is worth asking him/her to repeat what you said as they understood it.

If they get it right, fine, if not, repeat what you said earlier in a clearer way, so your partner understands you without any ambiguity.

It sounds simple, but it does work. You don't want to risk getting misunderstood by your partner!

You can learn more about How to Communicate Effectively on my Course: Legendary Love: _"How to Keep the Fire of Love Burning for Life"._

Connect with Your Partner Romantically Whenever Possible.

Use the "5 Love Languages" Suggested by Dr Gary Chapman.

1. **"Words of Affirmation".**

Find out if your partner likes your words of affirmation – like " I love you". "You look great" and other complimentary statements like that. Use them often if that pleases him or her.

2. **"Quality Time".**

Maybe your partner loves spending quality time with you. If that is case, make sure you create your "Together Time", when it's just the two of you together, talking, watching TV, or being out to watch a film, etc.

3. **"Giving of Gifts".**

If your partner appreciates little gifts of love like flowers, occasional affectionate cards, or anything else, then make an effort to give him/her these gifts once in a while.

33 | P a g e

Copyright © 2022.
Dr Grace Anderson.
All rights reserved.

4. "Acts of Service".

If your partner appreciates you doing some act of service for him/her, then do that as often as you can.

5. "Physical Touch".

If touching is your partner's way of feeling close to you, then make it a habit to touch him or her on the hand, shoulder, back, or wherever is convenient – lightly. Give each other hugs regularly and add words of affirmation.

For further exploration read The 5 Love Languages by Dr. Gary Chapman - (www.5lovelanguages.com)

INFIDELITY AND LACK OF COMMITMENT

Issues arising from Non-Commitment.

Is He Really Committed to You? Are You Really Committed to Him?

Commitment can be one of the scariest things that many men face in their lives. Everything is great as long as their girlfriends don't expect them to totally commit to them, and only them. There's just something about saying to someone that you'll be only with them from now on that strikes terror in the hearts of a lot of guys. It's because of this that it's difficult for many women to know whether or not their boyfriends are fully committed to them.

They certainly don't want to bring up the subject because that can end everything and send the guys running for the hills. So, the question becomes how can you tell if he's committed to you or not?

Looking at the way your guy reacts when you mention things such as weddings of friends or relatives, will give you a big clue as to how he feels about permanent commitment. If he turns pale and sweaty, you've probably got a man on your hands that would rather throw himself off a Hawaiian cliff, rather than get married. He also most likely will avoid the subject like the plague. You'll notice lots of subject changing.

Take a cue from the reactions you get as to whether or not you should simply sit him down and have a long honest heart to heart talk about where the relationship is going. If you get the feeling that he may become less interested in even being in a relationship if the subject is nailed down, you'll probably want to wait before bringing it up. This may be a difficult thing to do if you're ready for a full-blown commitment and he doesn't seem to be.

Another thing to notice is how he is around children, babies, in particular. If he doesn't seem to want to be around them and will do all he can to avoid this event, chances are good that he's not close to committing to you, or, probably, anyone else. Babies tend to frighten men that don't want a commitment because they see babies as the final nail in the coffin of entrapment. You see, babies are a true responsibility and it means that you're tied together for the rest of your life.

While guys may be amenable to moving in together, if they feel that you'll take this to mean that they're committed to you, it might not happen. Moving in with someone means that the relationship is being taken to the next level, that level being one where a commitment is involved. If they feel as if you're going to expect more from them with a live-in situation, they'll probably pass on it and insist that your relationship is more exciting when you each have your own places to call home.

Those are just the major ways of telling how your guy feels about commitment. On the other hand, if he loves talking about weddings, loves babies, and can't wait to move in with you, then you've got yourself a commitment in the making.

The same can be said of the woman in a relationship. If the lady never talks of the possibility of becoming engaged, getting married or having babies, maybe, long-term commitment is not on her mind. Some women just want to have fun and then move on to the next guy.

A lot will depend on whether what you have to offer her is "sufficient" for her to want to consider leaving her own job, for example, so she could look after your babies when they arrive, etc.

Again, set a convenient time to have a serious discussion about the issue of commitment, so that the two of you are sure where you are heading.

Has Anyone Had an Affair? If Yes, Should You Confess it?

Having affairs and cheating on partners is one of the most common factors that destroy relationships these days. Actually, cheating has gone on for as long as people have been attracted to each other. Both men and women are guilty of this, but it seems that men may have the edge on doing it more often. That may be because they say it really doesn't mean anything; that it's just sex.

Such men have no clue how insulting that is. Women are usually more emotional than men, so affairs aren't that enticing to them, except in cases where their partners are ignoring them and someone else has made them feel worthwhile and desirable.

As this goes on all the time, it seems, the question arises whether or not confessing to an affair is the right thing. There are a lot of variables in the answer to that question that keeps it from being cut and dried. For instance, if the person you've been having the affair with is someone you're in love with and can't see spending your life without, then you've got no choice except to confess to your current partner. You've probably already made up your mind to leave anyway, so you may as well get it over with.

From another perspective, if the affair was never really anything important, was very short, and is now over, it may not be necessary to confess to your partner. This is especially true if you've decided that your partner is the one you love. Confessing your indiscretion may end the relationship due to your partner no longer being able to trust you. It's certainly something to think about before rushing to your partner, confessing all, and begging for forgiveness on bended knee.

Some couples have what is commonly known as an **"open relationship"**. While this isn't necessarily the norm, it does work for many couples. In these relationships, you can most likely tell your partner all about someone else that you've slept with. They're probably going to tell you all about their extra--marital activities as well. This may actually be the extra exciting kink that jolts the relationship the way you need. However, it works for you if you're in that kind of relationship, there's no need to worry about confession.

One-night stands are another entity entirely. These things usually are drunken lust-filled mistakes and happened because of poor judgment. If this has happened to you, confessing may not be the best idea. But only you know your partner and whether or not they will be able to handle the truth. If you know that this is something that will never happen again, there may be no need to take a chance on losing a relationship that means a lot to you.

In the end, only your conscious can guide you in what's right or wrong in this. Just take into consideration all the mitigating factors before making your final decision. Remember, once you speak the words, you can't take them back.

The Need for Self-Discipline.

It is vital, in a relationship, to exercise self-discipline in whatever you do. That also applies to having affairs outside of your committed relationship. Betrayal of faith hurts and sometimes it hurts so deeply, the hurt partner is not able to get over it.

Whatever you do to your partner, be sure to understand that you could be jeopardizing your chance for true love and lasting happiness, if you deliberately do things that will hurt your partner.

So, apply self-control whenever and wherever you can.

CHAPTER 6.

HOW TO KEEP YOUR RELATIONSHIP HAPPY.

How to Strengthen Your Relationship.

Relationships are a difficult thing to maintain these days. Just look at the world around you right now; economy is falling through the floor, people are getting laid off right and left, and nothing seems to be going in the right direction. You have probably found yourself staying late at the office every night for the last two years, and your family is starting to feel like you don't even exist, until your pay check comes in anyway. There is a lot of stress out there in the world and there is a good chance that you are bringing some of that home with you.

Have Fun Together.

One thing that you are going to need to do to keep your relationship as strong as it was in the very beginning, is to plan one day a week where you and your partner do something fun together. It doesn't have to be anything extraordinary or super adventurous, but it should be something that the two of you enjoy doing together. Even if that is just sitting on the front porch reading a book, the key is doing it together and spending time with each other in a calm and relaxing atmosphere.

You may consider the time you spent with each other at night, before you both fall asleep in front of the television, as time together, but you need something that lasts a bit longer than an hour or so and without the television. You don't want to be distracted by something on the television when you are trying to spend time with each other. You should also make sure that neither one of you is on the computer, or on your Mobile Phone either. That has been known to cause a lot of problems in relationships, and you should always remember that, no matter what.

There are a lot of things that the two of you can do to spice up your relationship, so that neither one of you feels alone, even when you are together. Plan a date night and go out to dinner once a week. Sure, its sounds a bit odd, but you will be thankful that you took the time to sit down with your loved one and discuss the issues of the day with them. You might even find that it helps you relieve some of that stress that has been building up in your life and that is always a good thing.

Keeping a relationship strong is a difficult thing to do these days. A few decades ago, there wasn't as much technology and the pace of life was a bit slower. You could sit down at the dinner table and spend the rest of the night together talking and having fun. Today, your job can become a priority in your life and you might find that work is trying to call, text, and email you at all hours of the day and night. No job is worth ruining your relationship for, and you need to fully understand and accept that, in order to remain happy in your life.

Laughter Helps Relationships.

One thing that people seem to forget in their relationships is the fact that you have to have a sense of humour. There are going to be plenty of times in your lives together that you are going to need to laugh to keep your relationship going strong. Of course, you are going to have to figure out when the appropriate times are to laugh and when it's probably not such a good idea. After a few years of marriage, you shouldn't have too much of a problem figuring out those times, though.

Everyone feels better when they laugh. After all, **"laughter is the best medicine".** You just have to be able to find the humour in the moments that most people wouldn't. If you get upset when every little aspect of your life that goes wrong, then you are going to end up being a very angry person when you get older and you will probably be alone to boot. If only you would have laughed a bit more, you would probably be a happily married individual with a loving family. Instead, you are sitting in a nursing home bitching about the taste of the pea soup again.

Everything that happens in your life can have a funny anecdote to it. You just have to look hard enough to find one. Your relationship with your partner is going to have moments where nothing seems to go right, and everything is falling apart around you. Don't give up and don't give in to the anger that is building up inside you. Instead, you should find something to laugh about and get your partner to join in with you. Even if you have to sit down together and talk about funny things that have happened in your lives before you met each other.

Finding things to laugh about and enjoying the time you are sharing together will strengthen your relationship to the point that nothing can affect it. You won't have to worry about being upset and saying things neither one of you actually means and you can do more things together. **You can't live your life in a bad mood.** It's been tried before, and those people are never fun to be around. You have to make things in your life better for both of you and laughing is the easiest way of accomplishing that.

When things have got you down and there seems like there is nowhere for you to turn, just remember that you have a partner that is there for you. The two of you can work through any obstacles that beset you and you should always remember to laugh. Nothing is better than having a person that will laugh with you rather than at you, and your partner should be that type of person. When it comes down to it, you have to be able to give your partner your attention and your love, but you should also remember to give them your sense of humour anytime it may be needed.

The Role of Apology and Forgiveness.

Learn to apologise when you have done something to hurt your partner.

True apology means that you are truly sorry for the hurt you have caused your partner. It also means that you are pledging to desist from doing the same thing again. If you are truly sorry, your partner is very likely to forgive you.

If you are the one that has been hurt due to your partner's misbehaviour, try your best to forgive your partner. Forgiveness has the power to heal your pain much faster than anything else.

Commitment.

Most times, a committed relationship is a much happier than a non-committed relationship.

It is easier for you and your partner to plan your future together if you are both committed to your relationship. If you have no intension to commit to the relationship, it's best to let your partner know that as soon a possible so that they won't have their hopes dashed in the future.

In Chapter 7, we will look at the Role of Third Parties in relationships.

CHAPTER 7.

ARE THIRD PARTIES CAUSING YOU PAIN?

Social Media.

What is the role of social media in Your Relationship?

Don't Let social media Become the Third Party in Your Relationship.

Are you or your partner addicted to social media?

Are you always on Facebook, Twitter or Instagram?

It is okay to be on social media to connect with friends, but it is not okay to let it take over your life!

Do everything in moderation. Do not begin to copy what others do or say just because you want to "belong".

It would be irresponsible to fail in doing your normal chores just because you were busy following conversations on Facebook or on Twitter.

It would also be wrong to join groups that are not going to help your relationship flourish.

It is best to make sure that your partner is not just your romantic partner, but also your best friend! You have to try!

What Kind of Friends Do You Have?

Your friends can be a pain in your relationship if you allow them.

Some female friends are not always true friends. I once had a best friend who did everything, she could break up my marriage by telling me lies about what my husband was doing with other women. When the pain of her tales became unbearable, I banned her from ever communicating with me or my husband ever again. I broke up my relationship with her altogether.

Some men friends are exactly the same. They could go behind your back to try and seduce your girl and come back to tell you that your girl is too flirtatious or cannot be trusted to be faithful.

So, do watch who you are friends with. If you find they are no good, drop them!

Bad Habits.

What are your bad habits?

We all have one or two bad habits. What are yours? Is any of your bad habits causing problems for you in your marriage?

Gambling?

Do you gamble your money away every payday? Does your partner know that you are indulging in gambling?

If she knows that you have that problem, what have both of done to save you from this money-draining activity? Yes, it is true that you can have some wins once in a while. But if you were to take a good and critical look at the pros and cons of gambling, you will find that the cons outweigh the pros. So, STOP it as soon as possible before it ruins you and your family financially.

Consider the adverse consequences your gambling could cause you. Some people have been found to become homeless because of the huge financial losses they have suffered.

Yet some others have been known to commit suicide when they couldn't get themselves to stop gambling. Food for thought!

Do You Drink Your Senses Away Every Friday or Saturday?

Some partners have been known to make the Pubs their second home every weekend! Are you one of those?

Consider the harm alcohol could cause to your body and vital organs.

Here's what Wikipedia says about the effects of excessive alcoholism:

"Alcohol use can affect all parts of the body, but it particularly affects the brain, heart, liver, pancreas and immune system.[3][4] Alcoholism can result in mental illness, Wernicke–Korsakoff syndrome, irregular heartbeat, an impaired immune response, liver cirrhosis and increased cancer risk.[3][4][15] Drinking during pregnancy can result in foetal alcohol spectrum disorders.[2] Women are generally more sensitive than men to the harmful effects of alcohol.[10]".

That is clearly stated, and I am sure you probably know someone who is currently suffering from the alcoholism disease or diseases.

So, if you are affected by this, please do something about it straight away. Not only your life, but your relationship is also at risk.

Do you Go to Night-Clubs Without Your Partner?

Are you having fun with other people while your partner is alone at home? Are you excluding your partner from a certain fun activity because it gives you the freedom to flirt or become unfaithful?

Some men have the habit of going to nightclubs alone while their partners are at home alone looking after the children. They also have the tendency to have one-night stands with other women and come back home so late at night that their wives are either asleep or simply livid with anger!

Some women also do the same thing and return home very late and half-drunk.

Such a habit can easily break up your relationship. Be careful how you handle your relationship as any careless and carefree attitude and behaviour can give your partner ample reasons for a break-up of your marriage or relationship.

Do You Have a Stalker?

Stalkers are a menace and can cause a lot of grief to the person being stalked. Sometimes, stalkers are just crazy people who, perhaps, have never met you face to face, but have got in in their sick heads, that they "must" have you. So, they make it their duly to follow you around, send you unsolicited letters and messages, find out where you live and just make life generally miserable for you.

On other occasions, they could be your ex-boyfriend or husband/wife or someone you jilted a while ago.

Whatever the case, please report it to the Police as soon as you notice.

If on social media, delete your account on that platform.

Conclusion.

I have only mentioned a few of the serious distractions that could become the "third-parties" in your relationship. There are of course many more and only you can know what the issues are.

Hopefully, none of them applies to you. If, on the other hand, you have a tendency to do any of those things mentioned above, it is your duty to either pull away from that activity or indulgence, as soon as you can, or go out and seek help.

In Chapter 8, we will take a brief look at how Spirituality Can Help You in Your Relationship.

Chapter 8.

SPIRITUALITY AND RELATIONSHIPS.

What is Spirituality?

Dictionary.com defines Spirituality as follows:

"Spirituality has to do with the spirit, not as in ghosts, but as in the essence of being human — your soul or your inner life. Spirituality often has to do with religion, but it doesn't have to. You might say, "I'm not religious; but I have a strong sense of spirituality," which might mean that you practice yoga or meditation, or you pray with a group, or you nurture your spirit by spending time in nature. Religions usually have defined beliefs, rituals, and guidelines; spirituality is more individual."

So, are you or your partner spiritual in some way? If one of you is spiritual and the other one isn't, this could cause problems for you, unless you are both sensible enough to manage the situation.

Some Attributes of a Spiritual Person.

1.Being Considerate of other people.

A spiritual people try not to be selfish. They consider other people's feelings before they say or act in a certain way.

They try and "Love their neighbour as themselves", meaning they will try to do unto others as they would want others to do unto them".

So, if you were to apply that rule to your relationship, you will be trying your best not to do or say anything that will hurt your partner or your partner's feelings.

Spirituality also means Self-Preservation.

If you are spiritual, you will see it as your duty to preserve yourself as much as possible. That would mean that you will do your best not to self-harm by doing all the harmful things we already mentioned above like indulging in alcoholism or drugs, etc. You will find that when you keep your body and spirit healthy, your relationship will be truly rewarding and very happy.

Do You Belong to a Religion?

If you belong to any religion, you will find it helpful to find someone of the same beliefs as you while you are looking for a partner.

It will make life so much easier for you both when you have children. You can both teach them what you believe without any acrimony.

Unfortunately, many people pretend, while starting out to be the same religion as their date. Men are particularly guilty of this, although there could be women pretenders as well.

People's religions are very important to them. So, make sure you know what your date's beliefs are before you get seriously connected.

The Rule: "Do unto Others as You Would they Do unto You", still applies.

The above rule: **"Do unto others as you would they do unto you"** applies in relationships more than anywhere else. This is because you and your partner are regularly together.

If you like your partner to **serve** you in some way, make sure you find a way to serve them back.

You will need to apply **kindness** in your words and actions if you would like them to be kind in their words and actions as well.

None of you should be **"Lord"** who treats the other as **"Servant"**. Find a way to respect each other by your words and your actions.

The secret of ever-lasting love in a relationship is: **"Love, kindness and mutual respect for each other"**.

Find some time to chat with your partner over spiritual issues that may be bothering you. Discuss possible solutions and what part each of you can play in bringing spiritual harmony to your relationship.

The next chapter, the Conclusion will give you a brief overview of courses on Relationships and Self-Development that may interest you.

CHAPTER 9.

CONCLUSION AND ABOUT THE AUTHOR.

It has been my pleasure binging you this short introduction into "Relationship Issues: How to Find and Sustain a Great Relationship".

I do hope you have found my suggestions here really useful and will now apply some, or all of my suggestions, in finding someone to truly love and cherish for life!!

I wish you all the best!

Before you sign off, here are some of my other Courses, some of which you may find are either Complementary to this eBook, or are useful for your self-development.

Here are two Free Gifts for You:

1. 10 Questions to Ask On any Romantic Meeting - Free Report.

2. FREE REPORT: 7 Secrets For a Happy Marriage.
Check them out on: https://amazingsuccessacademy.com.

If you are Ready for a Comprehensive Relationship Course, then please check out this course below:

Legendary Love, How to Keep the Fire of Love Burning for Life.

This Course is a direct follow-up on this eBook. If you have already found someone to love or are already married, this Comprehensive Video Course – 5 Modules with 35 Lessons - will help you immensely, in keeping your love and passion alive.

Click on the image to check it out.

Still Looking for Your Soulmate?

How To Find True Love that Lasts For Life.

This is an Online Course That will walk you through in much more detail, the processes for finding Your True Love and making it last for life.

Click on the image to access this Course.

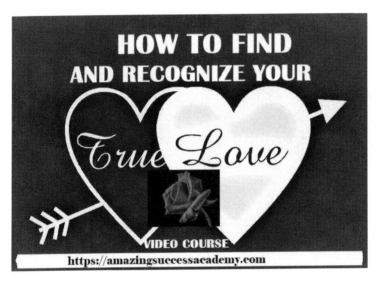

All Other Courses on:

https://amazingsuccessacademy.com.

All Enquiries to: Dr Grace Anderson.

Book Online on this link:

https://www.lifemasterymasterclass.com.

Make Notes.

Make a note of Your Dates – Record Your "Successes" and "Failures". Then Choose anyone you would like a second/third dates with and record your true feelings about how you think the friendship is going. Feel Free to create a Notebook in which you write the results of your dates until you find the one person that is most compatible with you and the one you would like to start a relationship with.

I met..

On..

The date went well because:

_____

_____

_____

_____

_____

_____

_____

_____

_____

_____

_____

MORE DATES.

Dates & Time	Who?	How Did it go?

Now, make notes on the person you would like to see again and one you would like to explore a relationship with. *Remember, don't expect perfection, no one is perfect, not even you!*

Name of My Preferred Person:	
Qualities that align with mine and what makes us Compatible	
1.	
2.	
3.	
4.	
5.	
6.	
7.	
8.	

Final notes.

1. Go out there knowing that you are the best of you around – no one else is exactly like you. So, hold your head up high and remain confident that the right person is out there for you.

2. Be as attractive as you can possibly be – without overdoing anything.

3. First few dates should be sexless – otherwise, your emotions will get you all confused. If you need to know someone really well, so that they could eventually become your life partner, then don't jump into bed with them until you have a good assurance that they are not just looking merely for a sex-partner.

4. Watch your drinks as they could be spiked - never leave your drink unattended. Throw it away if suspicious.

5. Avoid being in a secluded place with a man – if you are a woman – for your own safety. Only do this when you are sure that the man you are with cares about your feelings and cares about your safety.

6. Tell a friend or a family member of your dates – where you are going and who you are going with. Give a trusted person the Name, Photo and Telephone number of the person you are going out with. Stay safe!

Do You Need Coaching For:

- Your relationship?

-Your Mindset?

- Online Dating?

- Your Business?

Find out more below.

For more relationship Coaching by me, Dr Grace Anderson, please visit this website: https://lifemasterymasterclass.com and book your Free Discovery Session with me.

If you prefer to take an Online Course on Relationship Issues, Mindset, Confidence Boosting, etc, please visit:

https://amazingsuccessacademy,com.

Here's wishing you every good luck in finding your most compatible life partner!

See more about me on the next page.

ABOUT THE AUTHOR
DR GRACE ANDERSON

Dr Grace Anderson is a retired Teacher and Headteacher and now, a Certified Master Life Coach & NLP Practitioner. She specializes in Relationship, Mindset and Business Coaching.

Dr Anderson is also a published writer and novelist.

Websites:
https://drgraceanderson.com : -Various Services
https://www.lifemasterymasterclass.com : -Life Coaching Service
https://amazingsuccessacademy.com -Courses on Personal Development & Success Strategies
http://www.graceukalaswritings.com

Her novels etc: Including Dizzy Angel, (1985), The Broken Bond (2001) and Ada in London (2005). Dr Anderson's Other Books on Amazon: https://www.amazon.com/author/graceandersonsbooks

Printed in Great Britain
by Amazon